Reaching an audience online
A guide to digitally live streaming and webinars

Jack Versiani Holt
Kevin Brewer

Published by Versiani Holt and Brewer
For the United Benefice of Cradley with Mathon and Storridge /
Diocese of Hereford

First published in Great Britain 2018
Text © Jack Versiani Holt / Kevin Brewer
Cover design © HOLTOGRAPHY / *www.holtography.com*

All rights reserved. No part of this publication may be reproduced, stored in a retrieval system, or transmitted in any form or by any means, mechanical, photocopying, recording, or otherwise, without the prior written permission of the publishers.

ISBN 978-1-5272-2521-3

Under the 'Legal Deposit' scheme, this book will be deposited in the following libraries:

The British Library, London
The National Library of Scotland
The Bodleian Library, Oxford
The University Library, Cambridge

And if specifically requested by the following institutions:
The Library of Trinity College, Dublin
The National Library of Wales, Aberystwyth

Contents

About the authors — 1

Introduction — 3

What do you need? — 5
The internet connection — 6
The device (computer) — 7
Microphones — 7
In-venue amplification — 8
Live video streaming — 8

The live-streaming service / software — 11
How many people will the webinar tool accommodate? — 11
How much does a webinar cost? — 11
Can I record the live-stream / webinar? — 11
Can I stream a pre-recorded video? — 12
How is audio handled? — 12
How will people join the live-stream / webinar? — 13

Who else needs to be involved? 15
A technical person 15
A facilitator 15
In-venue helpers 15
Allowing interaction / questions from online audiences 16

Presentation planning & preparation 19
Plan the visuals for your webinar 19
Be prepared 20

Tips for a live presentation 23
Personal preparation 23
Audio preparation 23
Video preparation 24
Visual preparation 25
Presentation tactics 25

Ever changing technology 29

About the authors

Jack Versiani Holt

Jack completed a Masters Degree in Wildlife Documentary Production and has applied this learning in effective digital communications. In his profession, he has consulted on how to effectively communicate through digital outlets. Recently Jack was involved in a successful pilot project, presenting across a live-stream broadcast, allowing greater access to talks in rural Herefordshire.

Kevin Brewer

Kevin has worked extensively as a specialist in data connectivity, managing the delivery of complex I.T. projects in both the commercial and non-profit sectors. He sees the power of live-streaming technology as a positive force for good, bringing together communities and enabling participation in events by those who would not otherwise be able to take part.

Introduction

More and more people are offering access to live talks, presentations and lectures via a 'live-stream' over the internet, sometimes referred to as a webinar (an online-seminar). This widens the possible attendance of the event, allowing for easy participation for those who are unable to travel to be present at the event in person.

There is a certain amount of technology and equipment required and it is important to be well organised in advance, but with good planning and preparation it is not difficult to live-stream.

What do you need?

Exactly what you will need will depend upon the scope of your live-stream. If you are planning to live-stream your event, it's important to check in the early stages of planning that your venue has (or can support) all that you will need.

Things to consider include whether you need to present content beyond the one presenter's audio and visual presentation. This may include video-streaming live from the venue as the presentation is ongoing and audio/visual input from audience members within a Question and Answer Session (good examples of a more advanced broadcast setup include Question Time, BBC).

Here is a basic list of things you will need, followed by detailed consideration of each.

- **A reliable internet connection with sufficient bandwidth**
- **A device (computer / laptop) to conduct and broadcast the live-streaming of the event, with sufficient memory to record if needed**
- **Live-streaming / webinar software**
- **Microphone (fixed or portable) for the presenter(s) - connecting with the broadcasting device**
- **A digital projector, connected to the broadcasting device to present the slides and/or other content to the audience in-venue if required**
- **Extra portable Microphone(s) to capture audience members if required**
- **Video (camera or web camera) capable to live-stream with the broadcasting device**

The internet connection

The first thing to establish is whether your venue will have a reliable internet connection with sufficient bandwidth. How much bandwidth you need will depend upon what you are planning to stream and whether the connection is public / shared.

If you're going to be sharing 'presentation slides', carrying an audio feed and also a live video feed from the room (so the online audience can also see the audience's in venue perspective), then a bandwidth of at least 1 Mbps* will be required.

Internet Service Provider unit of measure for data transfer is mega bits per second, not to be confused with the unit of measure for file sizes (Mega bytes).

If your video stream is high definition (not normally required for webinars) then your bandwidth requirement will be more – how much more will depend upon how high a definition you are planning to stream.

If you are only going to carry audio and presentation slides with no video streaming then 0.2Mbps should be sufficient.

With a good strong 4G connection it is perfectly possible to run a full webinar live-stream using that as your connection to the internet, however this may prove to be an expensive option due to the amount of data being broadcast.

Remember that when streaming you are uploading information online, rather than downloading. These requirements refer to upload speeds, not download speeds. Be aware that most internet service providers provide faster download speeds than upload speeds, so it's best to check this out carefully.

The device (computer)

Check out the ports available on the device you plan to use and make sure that they are sufficient. The computer you use needs to have the right type and number of ports to be able to plug in audio and, if required, camera and links to in-venue presenting kit, such as a projector.

In some cases, you might also want to have a small screen in front of the presenter, so they can see what is being presented without needing to look at the presenting screen and so avoid turning their back on the audience.

Microphones

One or more microphones will be required to capture the audio. How many microphones you will need will depend upon what you are planning to do.

For a simple set up with one presenter and no audience interaction, one microphone for the presenter will be sufficient. If the presenter is to speak from a fixed position (e.g. a lectern/stand) then a fixed microphone should be fine. However, if the speaker is free to move around (within the view frame of the video stream camera if one is to be used) then a wireless microphone (e.g. a radio microphone, clipped to the collar or lapel) would be more appropriate for sound quality and mobility.
If there are questions from the audience or more than one speaker at a time, then additional wireless or fixed microphones may be required. Take care that if more than one wireless microphone is used the frequency at which they operate is compatible.

With just one microphone, it is still possible to take questions from the audience, however the presenter would have to repeat the questions being asked in person, so the online viewers could hear what is being asked. This may cause delay but would be appropriate for a smaller budget.

In-venue amplification

Depending upon the size of your venue you may also need your microphone(s) to feed into an amplification system. However this is not strictly necessary for a live-stream / webinar. If this is needed care should be taken that the microphones are never too close to the loud speakers / PA system in the room, as to avoid distracting feedback.

Once this level of complexity is required it is probably best to consult a sound engineer or someone with a good understanding of setting up audio systems.

Live video streaming

A good quality video-camera or web-camera capable of live-streaming via the computer will be required if you want to stream an in-venue perspective. The camera will need to be connected to the computer, so do consider the setup.

Full HD resolution is preferable to record in, but this can consume more bandwidth and more memory. If you are recording locally, rather than using an online recording service (offered by some live-streaming services), it is worth considering how much your memory cards can record from your camera and whether it is more suitable to live-stream and record in a lower resolution, so as to not overwhelm the internet connection during your presentation.

Careful thought needs to be given to where the camera is looking (the composition of the shot). The presenter needs to be close enough so there is good detail and not appear too small, but also far enough away to have some space to move and still remain in frame of the shot.

Zoom capability, or wide-angle lens, considerations might be appropriate depending on your venue, to choose an appropriate camera. Unless you have a skilled operator, it is recommended to keep a simple and constant frame on this perspective.

The live-streaming service / software

An online live-streaming service / software will be required. The cost, functionality and maximum online audience size vary widely between the different suppliers and solutions currently on the market, so it's important to take time to find the right package for your needs.

Outlined below are questions you should consider, when weighing up your software options.

How many people will the webinar tool accommodate?

Most tools and pricing plans set a cap on the number of participants.

How much does a webinar cost?

Some services are free (but these often have a very low limit on the maximum number of participants). Other services charge for web-streaming and audio separately, some charge per audience member per minute, whilst others charge a flat fee per live stream, per month or per year. If you want to record your live-stream this can sometimes cost more too, while other services offer this at no extra cost.

Can I record the live-stream / webinar?

If you want to record the live-stream so that you can watch it again later, or make it available to people to watch later online, then you will need to make sure the solution you choose has this capability.

If you are recording the live stream, what gets recorded? Some services record the presentation slides and the audio, but don't record anything else, others record more.

Services also vary as to how you then download or make available the recording. If you are recording, respect the copyright of any material used and any licenses that might be required to broadcast it …. and don't forget to ensure the intended recordings are recorded at the time.

Can I stream a pre-recorded video?

If you want to play pre-recorded video as part of the presentation / live-stream then you will need to check if the solution you are using can handle this and, if so, how. Sometimes it is necessary to share a URL link with your online audience, when the film is to be played in-venue, that they can follow to play the content from an online hosted file (e.g. via YouTube, Vimeo or from your own website). In other cases the pre-recorded video content can be played directly over the live-stream / webinar software / service from the computer used to manage the event. This is an easier solution for your audience and tends to provide a better, more seamless experience, however it tends to be slightly more expensive to use solutions that offer this functionality.

If streaming a recorded video whilst you are live-streaming, do consider the capabilities of your bandwidth as this can overwhelm the connection.

How is audio handled?

Most services offer integrated, web-streaming audio (voice over internet protocol- VoIP), which allows participants to listen to the presentation through their computer speakers or headsets.
Other webinar platforms require online participants (and sometimes the presenter(s)) to dial in to a special phone number, with the audio then being carried over the telephone network.

Many offer both options, allowing online participants with low bandwidth to listen to the audio stream via their telephone.

There are usually two options for providing telephone based audio streaming:

1. **A number, for which the audience member has to pay the fees charged by the telephone service provider** (e.g. BT)
2. **A free number, for which you or your organisation will usually pay a set fee per minute for each participant** (which can quickly add up with a high turnout!)

How will people join the live-stream / webinar?

There will almost certainly be a limited number of places on your live-stream based upon the streaming / webinar service / software that you are using. Some services will let you buy more places if you need them, while others have a fixed limit based upon the options you signed up for.

It maybe a good idea to set up a registration process for your live-stream. It is important to be confident that everyone expecting to be able to connect can do so, to provide a good audience experience. This process needs to be in place before you start marketing the live-stream event. Many live-stream services offer registration as part of the package, or you could use a separate online event booking or ticketing service.

For free events it is not uncommon for some people not to attend, whereas the attendance is often far greater for paid events – however people will have higher expectations when they pay. The higher the price, the greater the expectation of a well-produced live stream. It is reputationally important to manage expectations, but also to deliver a high quality experience regardless if you charge for viewing or not. Advertise your live-stream well (use social media, websites, e-mail, etc.), but be sure to follow data protection and privacy regulations for your marketing.

Who else needs to be involved?

It is usually necessary to have some additional people involved other than the presenter.

A technical person

A technical person to set up all the equipment, get the stream running and monitor the live-stream to ensure that everything runs smoothly. This person should also monitor audio levels to test online viewers can hear and that in-venue speaker systems are appropriately adjusted to the microphone system. This person may also deal with any messages from online audience members (such as 'I can't hear the audio'), and if that support is not available, it is important to make it clear to online viewers in advance.

A facilitator

A facilitator to introduce the live-stream and keep the online audience informed as to what is happening (announcements to reassure people that they are connected correctly and to standby for the start of the live-stream that will be starting in five minutes, or that there will now be a break for fifteen minutes after which the live stream will resume, etc). The facilitator may also introduce the presenter(s) and provide any additional or follow up information to those online at the end of the event.

In-venue helpers

In-venue helpers for example as 'microphone runners', if there are questions from the in-venue audience that need boadcasting within a large venue or for the live-stream.

The facilitator might manage this, ensuring that there is always a microphone near the person who is speaking, and additional 'helpers' may be useful to execute this type of task, equipped with wireless microphones.

A good example of this in BBC's Question Time are the helpers who do this when their audience ask questions to the panel.

Allowing interaction / questions from online audiences

Some live-stream / webinar solutions allow for the online audiences to respond to pre-prepared polls or votes, or to type questions / messages into a 'chat box', which can be seen in 'real-time' by someone managing this online feedback.

If the online audience can ask questions and interact during the event there needs to be thought given to how this will be managed.

Using a service that allows questions to be asked by audience members through typing them into the live-stream service 'message box' and having a moderator who can pass them to the facilitator, is probably the simplest approach.

Some live stream services do allow online audience members to contribute via audio (if they have a microphone enabled on their computer or are connected via a telephone network), however, this needs very careful management, to ensure only one person is speaking at one time.

Where this is possible, online audience members are nearly always all 'on mute' as default when the live stream starts. The technical person will need to 'un-mute' people who are to speak and then mute them again when they have finished. (Some webinar solutions allow people to click a button to highlight to the person managing the event that they wish to speak.) In this scenario it will also be necessary to amplify the incoming audio through the venue sound system so they can be heard in the room. This is beyond the scope of the purpose of this guide.

Presentation planning & preparation

Plan the visuals for your webinar

Because most presentations rely on audio and visuals to get the message across, both should be engaging. Slides with simple and appealing photography, with minimal text, generally work better in comparison to a lot of text.

Some slides you may wish to include are:

- **An introductory/cover slide to show before the presentation starts** (visible as soon as someone joins the event online), it could remind people what time the event will begin
- **A slide introducing the presenter,** including a photograph if available – especially if in-venue video streaming is not included
- **A quick overview of the agenda and the topics to be covered**
- **An ending slide that gives any further information about the presenter, future events or how to get in touch** (it can be a good idea to also include this in an email to online audience members when the live stream ends)
- **An intermission slide to show during any break scheduled** for the audience online, it's good to consider how their break is spent and could be used to reassure when your presentation will recommence

Be prepared

In order to give yourself the best possible chance of a successful event it is important to plan carefully and to be prepared.

- **Agree in advance a running order with exact timings for the presentation** (especially the start / end time and including any breaks that are to be included). It's important to stick to these timings so that the online audience know what is happening.

- **Agree the order in which people will speak, the exact duration of each speaker and how to transition between them** - if there is more than one presenter or speaker.

- **Set a deadline before the event for materials,** e.g. presentation slides - so that they can be loaded and tested on the device/computer to be used at the event, to ensure that they look and work as expected within the streaming software. (Never assume that the speaker will necessarily be using the same presentation software and equipment that you have on the day)

- **Test that all the technology in the venue works as expected.** It is a good idea to test this out well in advance and again just before the event.

- **Double check that you have everything on the day** (it's so easy to forget something simple, like the power cord for the laptop, which could bring a stop to the entire event). Arrive at the venue with plenty of time to set up and allow extra time to deal with the unexpected.

Tips for a live presentation

Personal preparation

Practice your presentation in advance, the more familiar you are with your talk, the more professional you can come across.

It is important to prepare notes and learn them thoroughly, as you may need to use them for reference. However, the more aware and confident you are of the prepared content, the greater the likelihood you will probably not rely much on the notes. This preparation can help keep notes to a minimum, allowing you to make a better impression with your audience.

Audio preparation

Allow sufficient time for you to become familiar with the audio equipment.

If you are using a lapel microphone, clearly you need to 'wire-up'. You should thread the microphone wires through your clothing (such as under the shirt etc.), so this set-up is discrete and not distracting to you or the audience.

It's good to have some help to finally clip/position the microphone in an appropriate position, but the most important thing is to be comfortable with the equipment you use. If the lapel mic doesn't feel natural and distracts you, try to relax and become familiar with it (as it may be the only equipment to hand); if you have the option, it may be better to opt for a regular microphone to hold, but this is entirely your preference.

Once wired up, it's essential to test the equipment is all working and that the audio levels are appropriately adjusted for all outputs (including the live transmission for online and the amplifiers in-venue). It is also highly recommended to take spare batteries for the microphones as wireless connectivity can consume a lot of energy.

When a talk is recorded through microphone, it is ever-more important to speak clearly and at a relaxed pace. You simply need to take the time to practice speaking with the microphone and allow a listener to feedback before you start the presentation.

An extremely important piece to prepare for is knowing how to mute your microphone at times when you are not presenting. Be sure to have the assistance or understanding on how to mute your microphone, as you don't want to mute when you're presenting or broadcast when you are taking a break.

Video preparation

If you have a live-video stream set-up within the venue, make sure to understand the frame your camera has set (if the camera is stationary). It is good to have reference points within the venue to help be aware of your position within the frame.

Good reference points mean referring your eyeline to certain stationary venue features that are easy to remember, which help keep you within the frame. If necessary, you can also mark your frame on the floor with tape, to feel when you are stepping out of shot. In general, it is good to try and limit your movements, so as not to be too distracting to your audience.

It is important to be framed centrally within the camera, so you have safe space in all directions to keep you in shot. It is also recommended to have the camera at eye-level: with the audience (if you want to gain the atmosphere of the room) or the presenter (to have a personal one-to-one shot).

Visual preparation

If you have a wireless device to click-through your presentation (such as a clicker or wireless mouse), be sure to have a fall-back. This may mean having a laptop open to use to click through, and within an appropriate reach of the presenter (so they are kept within the camera frame). If the device cannot be reached close to the presenter, technical assistance may be required.

If you have a break, it is good to prepare something visual for the screen to show during this time, especially for the online audience. Images and film (without audio) tends to be most appropriate and can be the best resource to hold your audience's attention. You could also design a subtle advert for people to tease what is to come next, clearly state the time of the break or simply show your contact details and such.

Presentation tactics

Don't over-think about the live-stream audience you are presenting to. The online audience will equally benefit from the attention you give to the people you are presenting to in person. Keep good eye contact with your audience, gauge their reactions and ensure your communication is clear.

Keeping eye-contact with the audience that is present is much more beneficial than keeping eye contact with the camera. Your online audience may not see the value with you staring down the camera whilst your presenting and it will detract from the experience for those in person at the venue. The only time that it may be appropriate to make eye contact with the camera, is when you answer a question from an online participant.

It is a good idea to explain to the in-venue audience that there is a live-stream of the event, so they build a good awareness.

Some feedback after live-streaming events suggests that the majority of in-venue audiences are either neutral about the live-streaming impact upon them, or feel that it actually enhances their experience, providing a feeling that they are now part of something bigger.

When you change slides, it is important to pause for a few seconds, as your live-stream may lag (transmit the audio and slide transition slightly behind time online). A slight pause will ensure that those online will see the new slide before you start talking again. Get into a rhythm and ensure you don't pause for too long.

There are no obligations to answer all questions that the audience may have. You can either set a time limit, or set a number of questions to be asked. Whatever you decide you need to be strict with your time, to abide by your overall schedule.

It's important not to let any one question consume all of your time. Do not give an extremely detailed answer. Decide in advance if you are willing to answer any outstanding questions after the event and make this clear with the audience.

If you do not have a mobile microphone for the audience in-venue, be sure to repeat the question so your microphone and online audience can pick it up. Answers don't make sense when the question isn't heard. This is also important if your online audience writes in with some questions, you will need to speak them for both the rest of the online audience and people in-venue.

If you are allowing the online audience to ask questions, it is recommended for them to submit by writing, and for you to choose top questions to answer (It could be helpful to have the facilitator or a moderator select the questions for you). Again, don't feel you have to answer everything, depending on how many are online you may be flooded with questions. It is good to set a limit here and make that aware to both your online audience and in-venue audience.

If things don't quite go to plan, don't worry, remain calm and carry on as soon as you can. Above all enjoy the experience. It is an exciting and rewarding opportunity to reach a wider audience who are able to enjoy your presentation at home/online, in addition to those in the room.

Ever changing technology

The authors have made every effort to ensure that the information contained within this guide is correct at the time of publication. However, computer based technologies can change quickly and new ways of working can be quickly introduced. For this reason this guide makes no reference to specific online products, services or companies, but instead focuses on the type of equipment and service someone planning a webinar will need. It is important to check out the current online companies and services at the time of planning your webinar, so as to be sure you pick the best one for your needs and budget.